Love On The Other Side
Heavenly Help for Love and Life

By Arielle Ford

Design: Colleen Taylor
Cover Art: Sharron Katz www.sharronkatz.com

Praise for Love On the Other Side

"Love on the Other Side proves how soulmates are not only found upon the earth, but also in eternity and offers compelling proof how love continues in the spirit world as demonstrated by Arielle's sister, Debbie Ford, who shares her profound spiritual wisdom from the other side."

~*James Van Praagh*
Bestselling Author of Ghosts Among Us

"An inspiring, heartfelt, and uplifting exploration of the eternal nature of love with real life experiences of love in the after life."

~*John Gray*
Bestselling author of Men Are From Mars, Women are From Venus

"Through a collection of dramatic stories of loved ones guiding us from the world beyond this one, Arielle Ford provides proof that Love On the Other Side is inclusive, not exclusive, and that the true nature of Spirit is that we are One."

~*Annie Kagan*
Bestselling author of The Afterlife of Billy Fingers

"A beautiful written book that explains how love transcends the earthly plane and expands into eternity."

~*don Miguel Ruiz*
Bestselling author of The Four Agreements

"Love On The Other Side is a deeply touching book that reminds us that our ancestors in heaven are always with us, loving us and willing to help us, all we need to do is ask."

~*Gabrielle Bernstein*
New York Times bestselling author of Miracles Now

"This sweet and soulful book captures the magic, mystery and endurance of love, and reminds us of the extraordinary help from on high that we have to create the miracle of love in our lives."

~*Katherine Woodward Thomas*
Bestselling author of Calling in the One

"Leave it to Debbie Ford to inspire a book while in spirit form. Love on the Other Side is a sweet, beautiful book that shares comforting stories about the enduring power of love. How wonderful to know that love (and our most treasured relationships) never die!"

Cheryl Richardson
Bestselling author The Art of Extreme Self Care

"Love on the Other Side provides the possibility, the proof and the pathway of connecting with beloved soulmates who have passed on. Through simple, engaging, beautifully uplifting and inspiring stories, examples and teachings, Arielle's book provides comfort and solace and a much-needed roadmap for re-establishing connection with our beloveds -- on Earth and in Heaven."

~*Sadhvi Bhagawati Saraswati*
Bestselling author of By God's Grace

"Expands our understanding of our eternal journey together through many lives and the miracle that we are never alone."

~*Victor & Wendy Zammit*
Bestselling authors A Lawyer Presents the Evidence for the Afterlife.

For my soulmate sister, Debbie.
Your love, light and brilliance continues to shine and bless me,
and all of us, who miss your skinny legs, laser guidance,
and simply hanging out having fun with you.
We know you are always with us.

Table of Contents

Introduction

It's funny how our priorities change as we age. Before I manifested and married my soulmate, Brian, my focus was on finding love. At that time I was 43 and single when I decided to make love my priority. I implemented every prayer, project, ritual and process I had ever used to create a highly successful business and aimed it, like Cupid's arrow, on the target called "soulmate love."

And it worked.

Brilliantly.

Once we married, my focus shifted to how to have a relationship that thrived and grew into a lifelong love affair.

Now, as I enter the last third of my life, I am looking at what happens to soulmate love after one of us transitions to the other side or what I like to call heaven.

The metaphysical student in me intellectually understands that "love never dies" and yet that thought doesn't really satisfy my curiosity of what happens when "love is on the other side."

Specifically, this book explores romantic love and soulmates and how that love continues beyond death.

Perhaps, most importantly for you the reader, it's a book about how your family (and friends) in heaven are open, willing and available to help you manifest a soulmate (whether your first or your fifth) on the earth plane.

The seed for this book began nearly two years ago as I sat with my dying sister, Debbie Ford. Debbie had dedicated her life to her global community of students (www.debbieford.com) teaching her groundbreaking work on "the shadow" and innovating the life-changing Shadow Process workshop. Along with raising her son, her work was her greatest passion and focus. During the last five years of her life, as she courageously dealt with a rare cancer, she found the will and strength to get out of bed and teach for a week and then would collapse for a month or more to rest up and generate enough energy to do it all over again.

At the end of her life she told me she had fulfilled her mission, that she had experienced a great life, and that the last year of her life, in spite of her weak condition and constant pain, had been the best year of her life.

Her only regret was missing out on experiencing a soaring, passionate soulmate love. In her final days, when she was awake, the conversation often turned to love and soulmates. In these pages I will share with you what she discovered once she got to the other side.

Additionally, there are several true stories about what happens when one half of a soulmate couple dies and how the love connection continues. This book will show how to make contact with your loved ones in heaven and ask them for their assistance. It will also reveal all the various ways our angelic loved ones are reaching out to us through signs, symbols, dreams and much more.

My deepest desire for this book is that it will eliminate any fear about dying that you, dear reader, may have, and that you will know that when your time comes, your loved ones will be waiting for you with open arms and open hearts and you will experience a burst of love greater than anything you have ever known.

Arielle Ford
La Jolla, CA

*"Without the density of her body,
I can better feel the intensity of her spirit."*

~Oprah (about her mentor and dear friend, Maya Angelou)

Chapter One
Losing Debbie

In a slow whisper I could barely hear, Debbie said:

"Sissy...do you think... I will meet my soulmate... on the other side?"

Wow. A question I could never have anticipated.

It was early evening as I sat next to my dying sister's bedside. We were in her bedroom, illuminated only by the light of a rising half-moon shining through her floor-to-ceiling loft windows, the streetlights of Little Italy, her San Diego neighborhood filtering through. Debbie had been sleeping most of the day, as she did every day as the cancer slowly took over her insides.

The woman who'd been a professional writer and speaker for most of her adult life spoke so rarely these days. Hearing her voice over the soundtrack of her labored breathing was a welcome contrast to the constant struggle to capture precious air, buoyed by the soft whoosh, whoosh of the oxygen machine hidden in her closet.

Now. This. Question.

Will I meet my soulmate on the other side?

"Yes, Debbie, of course," I said gathering as much certainty as I could in my voice. *"He's there… waiting for you. He can't wait to meet you!"*

My baby sister's eyes were still closed but I watched as she managed a small smile and fell back to sleep. Her question left me reeling, shaken and confused. Manifesting a soulmate is a subject I excel in. Books, workshops, online courses… this is my passion, my vocation, my gift; and yet, until this moment, I had never thought about the possibility of finding love in heaven.

I honestly had no clue if what I'd promised Debbie was true or not. But if just the thought of it brought my sister any comfort at all, then I was in one million percent.

Less than three weeks later she was gone.

The following days, weeks, months were an ever-changing tsunami of emotions.

One moment I was cool and calm, simply relieved that she was no longer suffering.

And then seconds later I would dissolve into a swampy, sweaty puddle of tears.

Sleep had been and continued to be a rare occurrence and I found myself haunted by her question.

Debbie's love life on earth had been a challenge for her.

Complicated. Chaotic. Sporadic.

She married a wonderful man in her late thirties and quickly gave birth to their son, Beau. She loved being a Mom but she and her husband had very different ideas about how their life together should look and they ended up divorcing before Beau was two. Fortunately they decided to become "the best co-parents" in the world to Beau and they succeeded. She even ended up writing her second book, Spiritual Divorce, based on what gifts and lessons she learned from the process of untangling their union. I really believe that the reason she and her ex-husband came together was to have Beau and show the world what's possible even when a relationship doesn't end with "happily ever after."

She deeply desired a loving relationship and yet she wasn't hyper-focused on finding a soulmate because she knew her number one priority was to be a great Mom to Beau, and with her very busy speaking, teaching and writing career, she didn't have enough time to devote to a relationship.

Now, at the end of her life, her desire for a deep, rich, romantic love life blossomed…would she find it in heaven?

"I know for certain that we never lose the people we love, even to death. They continue to participate in every act, thought, and decision we make. Their love leaves an indelible imprint in our memories. We find comfort in knowing that our lives have been enriched by having shared their love."

~Leo Buscaglia

Chapter Two
Love The Second Time Around

My amazing mother-in-law, Peggy, called me one day at the age of 80, announcing that she was ready for another relationship! Peggy had been married for fifty-five years, to a man named Wayne who had died years before. She'd spent the next five years as a widow, mostly doting on her all white, beautiful but neurotic Coton de Tulear dog, Noodles.

"How does a gal go about manifesting a soulmate?" she asked.

I started to chuckle to myself, shared the short version of my Soulmate Secret process and then added:

"And be sure to sign up for Match.com."

It was only a few weeks later that via the magic of the Internet, Peggy manifested a dapper widower named John. They quickly fell in love and spent the next several years together until John died at the age of 87.

After John's death, Peggy, feeling vulnerable and nostalgic, understandably ached to connect with her dearly departed men on the other side. I told her I'd help her do so, and arranged for her to do a phone session with a medium—one of my favorite intuitives—Laura Alden Kamm.

I had first met Laura a dozen years earlier, after the death of my stepfather whom we lovingly called Doc. Doc had died from pancreatic cancer in 2001, and during his final months, we often had very candid conversations about life after death, reincarnation and everything imaginable on this topic. Doc had assured me, that if he could figure out how to talk to me from "the other side," he would. Still, to be certain, we agreed upon "three secret words" that only the two of us would know. That would ensure I'd have "proof" he was really coming through.

Well, I got my proof all right, in the most incredible way. I'd previously connected my mother with Laura, who came to her home for a session. I joined the two of them toward the end of the hour, and was pleased to see that Mom seemed very comforted and happy with the messages she'd been receiving from Doc via Laura. I sat down next to Mom on her sectional sofa and asked Laura to see if Doc could reveal one of our "secret words." She closed her eyes, paused for nearly a minute and then her mouth seemed to tighten into a grimace and she said, "I'm not sure I can. I see him scribbling on a piece of paper but I can't make heads or tails out of what he is writing." I burst out laughing! Mom and Laura just looked at me like I was a lunatic.

"Laura, stop worrying, you nailed it," I said. "One of our words was griffonage, which Doc told me means unintelligible hand-writing!" There was no doubt in my mind Doc was with us. The rest of the session was a lovefest.

Soon it was Peggy's turn to enter Laura's magical world. We set a date for the phone call. A few days before the session, I started getting a bit nervous.

Unlike Wayne—Peggy's husband—John was very much a "believer" in the mystical realms. He wasn't shy and I realized there was a good possibility that he would dominate Peggy's session with Laura. Knowing that Peggy had her hopes on connecting with Wayne, her sisters, and several others, I called Laura to warn her that she might have to heavily manage their time together.

Laura laughed when she heard why I was calling. She told me that she had been hearing from "John" from the first moment Peggy's appointment was booked and she'd already told him that she will deliver messages from him but that he couldn't dominate the session with his constant chatter.

Being curious and nosy, when Peggy's session was over, I called to get the lowdown. She shared with me that she'd received clear messages from everyone she'd hoped to connect with, and she was nearly giddy with excitement as she shared that both Wayne and John professed their love for her. John had always been very attentive and affectionate but Wayne had been more reserved, stoic and less emotional. Hearing how much her husband of fifty-five years loved, adored and respected her brought her much joy and a deep sense of pleasure.

Which got me thinking: Peggy. Has. Two. Soulmates!

Two soulmates?!

Did I mention that there were TWO?

Which led to my next thought:

Then what will happen when she gets to the "other side?"

Will she be with Wayne or John or both?

I had no clue….until I set up another reading with Laura Alden Kamm in April of 2014. During this session I posed the question:

"Who will Peggy be with when she gets to heaven, Wayne or John?

Laura shared with me that Wayne immediately stepped forward, with John by his side and said:

"Both John and I will be here for her. John is in agreement. It's a shared love. "We are both attracted to the wholeness of her soul and her light. Each of us fell in love with a different aspect of her essence. Like a diamond, there are different facets that we fall in love with, soul to soul." There is no jealousy or envy between us because here we have evolved as souls."

Wow. I admit I was a bit surprised. While John certainly used this kind of language and was "into" this sort of thing, Wayne had been a highly recognized trial attorney, allergic to all things religious and spiritual. So, to hear him speak this way was so heartwarming! All I could think was, "Yay for Peggy!"

And, what about Debbie? Could my sister really find—or, perhaps had she already found— the soulmate relationship she longed for so deeply here on earth, there, on the other side?

I should pause here to say that I'm obviously open-minded by nature. I've always believed in life after death and reincarnation. Even as a young child this was a part of my inner knowing, born of personal experience.

16

One night, when I was seven years old, I woke up in the small bedroom that I shared with Debbie in Hollywood, Florida. I could see stars outside my bedroom window, and the house was very still and quiet. As my eyes adjusted to the inky darkness I saw a faint outline of a man sitting on the edge of my bed and I could feel a warmth radiating from him to me. Somehow I "knew" it was my Grandpa Lou, who was easily my favorite human. We had a grand mutual love for each other and every weekend he would create special experiences for me, including putting me to work in his watch repair business. We would sit, side by side on wooden stools, as I assisted him in taking apart the watches and putting them back together again. After work we would go out for lunch, usually hamburgers and Birch "Beer" at Royal Castle in downtown Miami. We walked along the busy downtown streets, holding hands, discussing whether we should spend the rest of the day at the zoo or the beach.

Now, here was Grandpa Lou sitting on my bed in the middle of the night. In his gentle loving voice I heard him say to me: "I'm going away but I will always be with you."

I instantly understood, and surprisingly wasn't afraid. A moment later the phone rang, lights went on, I heard my mother cry out and Grandpa Lou vanished. Some time later my father walked into my room. When he saw that I was awake he said: "Honey, Grandpa Lou has died."

"Yes Daddy, I know. He was just here and he told me."

Throughout my life I have always felt blessed to have my beloved Grandpa Lou hovering around me, looking out for me, and being a totally awesome guardian angel.

The French don't say 'I miss you.' They say "tu me manques"
which means "you are missing from me."

Chapter Three
Send Me Someone

These days, I begin each day sitting in my big, white bathtub gazing out over our spectacular ocean view. The combination of the fragrant lemony bathwater with our sea view calms my soul and sparks my creativity. One sunny morning after Debbie's passing, as I found myself soaking and thinking about whether or not Debbie was dating in heaven, I began pondering what happens with soulmates once one or both of them get to the other side? I had no idea I'd ever write anything on this subject, but a story I'd heard more than a decade beforehand from my friend Diana Wentworth, bubbled up in my memory. It went like this…

Diana was blissfully happily married to her soulmate Paul. Everyone loved their story, something that had been covered in magazines touting them as "one of the most romantic couples in Los Angeles." They'd raised a daughter together, merged their careers as founders of a weekly breakfast forum called The Inside Edge (www.InsideEdge.org), and had just celebrated their 25th anniversary, when Paul was diagnosed with terminal cancer.

To Diana's shock and horror he passed away only a few months later.

On his deathbed he looked at Diana and said, *"I don't want you to be alone."*

"Then send me someone," she said.

"I will!" he answered.

About two months later, Diana was hosting a breakfast meeting when a new member approached her. His name was Ted. As they developed a friendship he invited her out to dinner. She thanked him for the offer, but explained that she'd only been a widow for a few months.

"I'm just not comfortable going out on a date yet," she said.

Ted didn't press.

"That's okay. Here's my phone number. If you ever want to have breakfast, lunch, dinner, or tea, I'd love to get to know you."

After many phone conversations Ted was proving to be a warm, supportive friend she cared about deeply. Eventually Diana invited Ted for tea. Tea led to lunch. Lunch led to dinner. And they began to date.

One evening Ted and Diana were walking through the jewelry section of a department store. For the first time in his life Ted heard a voice speak to him. And the voice very clearly said, *"Buy Diana those earrings."*

Ted was completely startled, having never experienced such a voice, not to mention the urgent feeling that accompanied it. He saw before him a rack of tacky daisy earrings in many different colors.

Ted, a wealthy attorney, thought to himself, *"I would never buy anybody those ugly earrings,"* but the voice yelled at him.

"Buy Diana those earrings," it demanded.

So Ted pointed and said, *"Diana—those earrings!"*

She looked over casually and said, *"What earrings?"*

"Those daisy earrings," he said.

He noticed Diana was looking like she'd seen a ghost.

"Which ones?"

"The white ones with the yellow centers!"

With tears in her eyes she asked, *"What about them?"*

He said, *"Paul wants you to have those earrings!"*

It took a few moments for her to calm down. She was eventually able to explain that Paul had bought her an identical pair when they were first married. They had been her favorites and Paul had repaired them over and over for years until they finally fell apart. She had nearly forgotten them.

Those daisy earrings became one of several magical ways Diana was certain her first husband had kept his promise. Diana wrote a romantic memoir titled **Send Me Someone** and sold the film rights to the Lifetime Network. Diana and Ted have now been happily married for 25 years.

So much has been written about near-death experiences, the stories about going through the tunnel of lights into the arms of our ancestors and loved ones, but Diana's story was the first one I had ever heard that highlighted the possibility that our departed ones could actually intentionally improve our life by "sending us someone."

As I finally got out of the tub that morning considering all these possibilities of soulmates and heaven, I felt as if champagne was coursing through my veins. It was a feeling of lightness and brightness, a vast expansive feeling of eternal love. Wow. In all of my studies, mystical friendships, and teachings, I'd never heard much on this magical realm of possibility—the idea that loved ones on the other side could actually be intervening actively on our behalf back here on earth—and I couldn't wait to dig in and learn everything I could.

"I close my eyes and speak to you in a thousand silent ways."

~Unknown

Chapter Four
Ride The Wings of My Love

"Soulmate" is a word that has different meanings for different people. I believe that a soulmate is first and foremost someone you can completely be yourself with, someone with whom you share unconditional love, and when you look into their eyes you have the experience of being "home."

If you accept that definition then you can see that we all have many soulmates in our lives – not just our romantic partner but also, possibly, our children, parents, siblings, friends, co-workers, even our pets!

Here are two other soulmate definitions I really think are accurate:

"A soulmate is someone who has locks that fit our keys, and keys to fit our locks. When we feel safe enough to open the locks, our truest selves step out and we can be completely and honestly who we are; we can be loved for who we are and not for whom we're pretending to be. Each unveils the best part of the other. No matter what else goes wrong around us, with that one person we're safe in our own paradise. Our soulmate is someone who shares our deepest longing, our sense of direction. When we're two balloons, and together our direction is up, chances are we've found the right person."

~Richard Bach

and

"A Soulmate is an ongoing connection with another individual that the soul picks up again in various times and places over lifetimes. We are attracted to another person at a soul level not because that person is our unique complement, but because by being with that individual, we are somehow provided with an impetus to become whole ourselves."

~Edgar Cayce

As I began to think about the soulmate couples I knew, or had heard about, where one of them was now on the "other side," I decided to check in with them and find out about their experiences. I wanted to see if indeed, their departed partner has "sent them someone."

One of the biggest myths around soulmates is that we each only get one big love in a lifetime. This is simply not true. We all have many, many possible soulmates in every lifetime.

When your soulmate is on the other side you may doubt that you can ever love again, or you might feel guilty even thinking about it, but our loved ones on the other side truly do want us to be happy and loved.

Kristine Carlson, widow of the internationally bestselling author of Don't Sweat The Small Stuff, Richard Carlson, has graciously shared her amazing story of love from the other side:

Nestled in the rolling foothills of the Santa Monica Mountains, the Malibu campus of Pepperdine University overlooks a majestic view of the Pacific Ocean. The breathtaking vistas from Pepperdine have a magical quality to them and it was here that magic conspired to bring two soulmates together.

Richard Carlson and his best friend Rich, were walking through the Pepperdine cafeteria in October 1981 when lightning struck. Richard's eyes fell upon a beautiful freshman, Kristine, who seemed to know everyone in the room. Spellbound, he watched her move from table to table, greeting everyone with her warm smile and open nature. He told his pal Rich, "This is the girl I want to meet!"

Even though Richard was considered very friendly, the truth was he was quite introverted and painfully shy and just wasn't ready to make a move.

As fate would have it, a few days later, on a Sunday, Richard and Rich were walking on campus, and saw Kristine at a distance. She noticed them checking her out and knew they wanted to meet her so she walked over to them. Rich, decided to take off while Richard and Kristine spent the next three hours sitting under a weeping willow tree talking.

The conversation flowed and Kristine recalls feeling "super comfortable, very much at ease and happy to be with him."

Afterwards she called her Mom and had their normal conversation…including the typical Mom question, *"have you met anybody?"*

Kristine shared, *"Yes, Mom, I think I just met the man I am going to marry!"*

Her Mom laughed and asked immediately, *"Have you gone out with him yet?"*

"No, I only just spoke to him this afternoon."

Mom suggested, *"Maybe you should go on a date first!"*

Richard and Kristine finally saw each other again three weeks later at a dance on campus. Although both of them already had dates for the event, they eventually found themselves dancing together.

"The moment we touched we both felt an explosion of energy and we instantly fell in love." Kristine said. *"I remember thinking, I've known him forever."*

Kristine never expected to meet the love of her life just weeks after leaving home for the first time. In fact, she fully expected to meet "the one" much later in life, and she already had a very long priority list of what her soulmate would be like!

But there was something about Richard….she just knew they were meant to be together and Richard's qualities exceeded her list by a long shot.

They were rarely apart. Richard was studying political science and business. Kristine focused on communications and advertising. In her senior year they took a Valentine's Day ski vacation in Vail. While on the ski lift, Richard proposed and of course, she said YES without any hesitation!

On August 31, 1985 they married in this exquisitely beautiful garden of a charming hotel at Oregon's Columbia Gorge, the windsurfing capital of North America. Magic was once again dancing by their side…during the ceremony the wind completely stopped and all their candles stayed lit. At the end of ceremony, the wind was back up at full speed. Nearly everyone noticed this very unusual and auspicious occurrence.

Although Kristine had grown up in Beaverton, Oregon, they settled in Northern California near Richard's hometown of Piedmont. By then Richard had realized that he was really a healer at heart. He studied Rolfing and then committed to earning his Ph. D in psychotherapy. He joined a cutting edge group dedicated to "happiness training and stress management." They had two daughters, Jasmine and Kenna and life was good.

"Richard was always so magical and light... he was wonderful to live with and fun to be with," Kristine recalls. "We only had three arguments in our 25 magnificent years together." She often told her friends that she needed more than one lifetime to love him.

Both were devotees of the Indian Saint, Sai Baba and they shared many mystical experiences together. Richard often had intuitive dreams ranging from knowing who would win the World Series to seeing which slot machine to play in Reno or Las Vegas. One time he won $10,000 at a slot machine and when all the bells and whistles went off, he was deeply embarrassed by all of the unexpected attention.

Richard became famous with his 10th book, that became number one on the New York Times list for over 100 weeks, ***Don't Sweat the Small Stuff...and it's All Small Stuff.*** People magazine once named him one of the **"Most Intriguing People in the World."**

In 1999 Richard had another prophetic dream...he dreamt that he died on an airplane. As a busy author who traveled the world quite a bit, this dream created some anxiety for him about flying. Seven years later, on December 13, 2006, he had a blood clot during the descent of his flight into New York and died on the plane.

His sudden death was a shock not only to Kristine and her girls but also to Richard. She intuitively knew that Richard was confused about what had happened to him and where he was. He really didn't know he had passed and Kristine could feel his agitation and upset. She kept telling him to go to the Light, to find Baba's feet and Baba would tell him what had happened.

Through friends she connected with a medium, who didn't know anything about Richard, and yet she was able to share with Kristine and the girls intimate details she couldn't possibly know.

"During the session I felt him hug me, and I sensed a warm orange glow while he transmitted energy to me with a request to carry on for him, he asked me to keep writing in spite of my previous resistance," she said.

The first two years after he crossed over Richard was a constant presence. Late at night, Richard's spirit would wake her up and he began to communicate where he was and what he was doing. During the days he also found a way to come through her while she typed at her computer.

He shared that all the teachers of love had to amp up what they are doing…with more energy, greater clarity because the world was in dire trouble….he spoke of a negative energy pulling the earth into a bad position and said it would take love to restore the earth to its natural status which is love, because the fear is so great.

Right after his memorial service, his dear friend Ben was sitting with Kristine on the floor of her home, holding her hand. While they were sitting there, Kristine looked up at Richard's office and saw a very bright round pulsing light on the wall. She asked

Ben, what he thought it was and he said "that is a human heart." They watched it for a minute and then it disappeared....

Ben said, *"Richard must really be having some fun with this!"*

"Yes," she agreed, *"and it's totally Richard expressing his heart and love for both of us."*

Later that day Kristine got a call that her book would be published. The book was originally a 35 page letter Richard had written and given to Kristine for their 18th anniversary. The book was titled **An Hour To Live An Hour To Love, The true story of the best gift ever given.**

Gifts from Richard were appearing in all kinds of forms.

Kristine believes that she and Richard were one spark that became two....she feels that there isn't a separateness to them.

"Love transcends the boundaries of time and space. Love truly never dies with the body. That is what is eternal...the deeper connection you have of love in life, the deeper you experience that love forever. The only reason we are separated in form at all is ego. I know that Richard and I are twin flames."

She misses laughing with him and she remembers that when they were together she was always trying to memorize his face.

"There isn't any real death. It's just a word. There is a journey. We are both very much on our journeys and he comes back and visits me. He comes to me in dreams. I chase him down and find him in a hammock. I ask him, 'Where have you been?' He says, 'I've been here all along.'"

Today she is now in a relationship with Randy.

"We are soulmates of a different kind."

They met eleven months after Richard passed and over the years have spent quality time together and have now been exclusive during the past two years.

"Richard sent him to me so I would be happy and not suffer."

She describes her relationship with Randy as "very different" from her relationship with Richard. Kris doesn't know what their future holds, but he fulfills the "fun factor" of life for her.

"Randy allows me to live a life of joy amidst a very heavy work schedule. I love him and he's very loving. He cooks for me while I drink champagne and I can talk about Richard all I want. He is totally okay with it and often jokes that in some ways we are a threesome!"

Randy's friends often ask him how he can be 'ok' stepping into this "big man's domain" and Randy says, *"I never try to replace him, I know I have a different relationship with Kris. She has the best of all worlds."*

Randy also had an experience with Richard. One day, when he got into his car, he felt a presence and he had a very vivid and telepathic moment where Richard told him that Kris deserved his honesty.

Today, for Kristine, the communications are much subtler… although she still feels he is always with her….his essence is deeply within her. Since he has passed she thinks about him many times a day and sometimes asks him to be present for their daughters when they need extra love, care and support.

When she dies she has arranged to have her ashes mixed with the remaining half of Richard's ashes. When she gets to the other side she fully expects to walk right into his arms. He has told her *"make the most of your short period of time on earth, have fun and breathe it all in."*

She always sees angel wings in the clouds when she looks up into the sky and she knows they are from Richard.

He tells her *"ride the wings of my love and I will take you home."*

Isn't that simply beautiful?

Here is poem Kristine wrote about the love she shared with Richard:

Soulmates

In the beginning We were one spark that became a single flame~

We danced and burned bright in our union and name~

And then God commanded us to separate and become two

For our soul work to take form and evolve Through all that we could learn and do~

The Yin, The Yang The Masculine and Feminine~

We parted with a promise:

I know that I am you and you are me. And we will remain connected through eternity~

I am, now, once again, but a spark without you, I will walk the earth half a soul until I find you~

I will wait as long as it takes

Knowing that you are there~

Instantly, we'll recognize each other again

We will burn as bright as the sun

Dancing and playing as one~

Creating great magic and harmony together

Our path is happy Full of Love and Light~

We will give hope

Others will follow as we roam~

Teaching that together we are a team, A partnership that conquers ego in Love~

A single candle with one flame Again burning bright~

Until our God expires half and leaves me to find Your spirit in mine~

My soul feels temporarily lost until I remember~

It is impossible to extinguish the divine.

-- Kristine Carlson

"Those we love don't go away, they walk beside us every day. Unseen, unheard, but always near; still loved, still missed and very dear."

~Anonymous

Chapter Five
Second Chances

Soon after speaking with Kristine, I spoke to Christina Rasmussen who had also lost her soulmate and, is now happily married to a new soulmate! Her magical, inspiring story is below.

On a beautiful winter night in 1996, Bjarne and Christina met at a party when she was in Bjarne's home country of Denmark as an exchange student. He was tall, handsome, blond hair, blue eyed. Christina is a Greek born dark haired beauty.

They arranged to meet the next day but he never showed up.

She instantly felt something was wrong and *"I moved heaven and earth to find him."*

She was shocked at her drive to find him but just knew she must. She had an inner conviction that they were supposed to be together.

By calling friends, and friends of friends, she discovered that he decided not to show up. When they finally connected he begged her for another chance and she agreed to make a date with him.

Ten days after their first official date she told her parents she had met the man she would some day marry.

On a rainy summer day, August 8, 1998, they married in a picturesque church in the town of Aarhus, Denmark, with 45 friends and family surrounding them. They spent their honeymoon in the Canary Islands, madly in love with each other, and by the time they got home, Christina was pregnant. Their happiness was short-lived.

Tragedy befell them when their baby girl died at birth. To heal and overcome their grief they decided they needed to go on an adventure and ended up moving to Houston, Texas.

Life in Houston was very different. Her husband found a career that he enjoyed but because of her foreign status, Christina wasn't allowed to work. She was soon pregnant and their daughter Elina (now 14) was born healthy and beautiful.

After a few years they realized that the weather in Texas was just too hot for them and they decided to move to San Jose, CA. Two years later they had a second daughter and they were now a very happy family. They loved the life they had created and spent their time together biking, hiking and enjoying the California lifestyle.

In early 2003, Bjarne received a great job offer in Boston and they moved cross country for yet another adventure.

Soon after arriving in Boston, Bjarne noticed a growth on his neck. He went to the doctor who said his blood tests were "perfect," but the next day, when the biopsy results of the growth came back, he was diagnosed with stage four cancer. Three and half years later he lost the battle.

After eight blissful years of marriage and two beautiful children,

Christina was all alone, overcome with grief at the loss of her soulmate.

During the last months of his life she asked him over and over again not to leave her. When he was dying, she was sitting on his bed and he said to her:

"Listen to me my love. One day you will meet this really amazing guy for you and the girls. Only the first two years after I go will be really hard and then everything will be ok."

She was so afraid of living without him. Once he had crossed over, she found that she couldn't sleep unless the lights and the TV were on.

Nine days after Bjarne passed, Christina noticed that her Bose speakers began turning on all by themselves, even though they were unplugged. Sometimes lights would turn on. Doors would blow shut even though none of the windows were open to create a breeze. Loud, strange noises would occur. Her parents, who were staying with her at the time, could see and feel Bjarne in the house, as did her sister. They began to tell Christina that she needed to sell the house and move so that she wouldn't be afraid.

"Bjarne loved this house and was such a big part of it that I felt that I couldn't leave. I felt I needed to find a new way to live and raise our girls."

Bjarne occasionally made himself known. Four months after he died she awoke in the middle of the night and saw him standing near her in a white T-shirt and jeans. She said out loud, *"Oh my God. Oh My God. Oh my God"* and then he disappeared. Two years later their babysitter (a 40 year old teacher that worked for them for years) was at the house, sitting on the couch. She saw a man standing in front of her and thought it was a burglar until she recognized that it was Bjarne.

In spite of these appearances, Christina's grief was intense.

"When he died, I died. My heart was completely broken. I believed I would never love again. I became mean and bitter and I suffered so much."

Fifteen months after Bjarne's death, Christina took her girls to a support group for children who had lost a parent. It was there that she met Eric, whose wife Pam had died suddenly seven months earlier at the age of 35.

Christina had told her friends that she would never have to look for another spouse because the one meant for her would just sit down next to her. That is exactly what happened at that support group.

While she and Eric were falling in love, she was still also in love with Bjarne. He was her everything. She was still talking to him constantly.

"When I met Eric, I felt sick to my stomach because I liked him but I felt frozen. I felt guilty about dating or even wanting to meet someone else. I slowly remembered that Bjarne had told me I would meet someone, I think he even said he would "send him to me." As I came to know Eric I realized that Bjarne and Eric couldn't be more different. Eric is a true earth angel and Bjarne sent me someone who is exactly what I needed!"

Two years later they married.

"I really believe Bjarne sent Eric to me and the girls….they adore their step-father."

One of her daughters recently said to her:

"I feel guilty that I don't think about Daddy every day. I feel guilty that I love Eric."

And Christina explained to her that "you have a Daddy in heaven and a Daddy here and your Daddy in heaven wanted it this way."

Today she still loves Bjarne as much as ever. She still misses him every day. She looks at his photos and he is an integral part of her daily life. And the love she feels for her second soulmate, Eric, is huge but yet different and she has a heart big enough for both of them.

She once had a dream where Bjarne came to her and said "you are doing the work on this side and I am doing the work on my side and we were meant to do it this way."

Christina believes that when Eric and she are on the other side, she thinks she will be with both of them, although Eric isn't quite ready to accept that.

"We are meant to be part of a group and we will all be together. I have two soulmates. The heart can love many times in many ways as we are here to love more than once. One soulmate is in heaven and one is here with me. I am so fortunate and I love them both so much," Christina concludes.

I think Christina is right. The heart can love many times, in many ways, and we are here to love more than once.

The idea that we each only get one big love in a lifetime is a myth. You could call it a big, fat lie.

I don't know where this idea/myth originated but I know that it simply is not true. I know several people who have had more than one soulmate in this lifetime. Some married their soulmate only to divorce many years later. Does this mean they were never soulmates?

No.

Some relationships come with an expiration date.

And then the possibility exists for you to manifest your next soulmate!

I now understand that sometimes your soulmate on the other side can and will assist you in meeting your next soulmate.

And, it could happen faster than you ever expected!

"When someone you love becomes a memory, the memory becomes a treasure."

~Unknown

Chapter Six
Our Hearts Are Big Enough to Love More Than One

I'll never forget the day I met Steve Amos. It was 2002 and we were sitting in a red leather booth at a local bistro having BBQ turkey burgers and fries for lunch as we discussed all the various people that we knew in the self-help and spirituality market-place.

I noticed that Steve talked about his wife, Terri. A lot.

He was obviously madly in love with her and very proud of her as a wife, woman and a mother. Near the end of our lunch, as he was again singing Terri's praises, he mentioned she had once been Miss USA. And that's when the light bulb went on!

"Oh my God Steve, you're not married to Terri Utley are you?" I was nearly shouting.

"Yes, do you know her?"

I told Steve how I knew his beloved wife. Way back in 1983, one of my jobs included promoting the Miss Florida USA pageant for a tourism department in Fort Lauderdale. That was the year Miss USA, Terri Utley, was the hostess of our live televised pageant. Terri and I met and spent a few days working together. Afterwards we stayed in touch and a year later we both ended up living in Los Angeles. Terri was launching her career as a broadcast journalist and within a few years was hired for an on-air position in another state and we lost touch.

Steve was just amazed to hear this and he quickly called Terri and then handed me the phone. I was thrilled to reconnect with my old friend! Before long, we planned a lunch for the following week. I brought my husband Brian, Steve brought Terri and it was a delightful gathering.

I continued talking to Steve about various joint ventures on a fairly regular basis, even after he and Terri moved from Southern California to the Florida panhandle.

And then Steve became harder to reach as he turned most of his business matters over to his partner due to the fact that he was recovering from prostate cancer. We eventually completely lost touch.

Then one day a mutual friend called to tell me Steve had died.

Suddenly.

Of a heart attack.

He was only 56.

Terri never saw it coming.

She had been away for the weekend attending her daughter Kolbi's dance competition. As they were driving home from New Orleans, her other daughter Mackenize called to say her Dad was more than a half hour late picking her up and even though she called him repeatedly, she couldn't find him. Terri then tried to reach Steve and couldn't. She called her neighbor Jen and asked her to see if she could find out what the delay was.

The call back from Jen was devastating. Steve was dead.

That night as she sat in her neighbor Jen's home, waiting for the police to finish their investigation, she decided to ask Steve's spirit to speak to her. As she sat in Jen's bathroom, the room became a blur. She felt Steve's presence with her and clearly heard his voice in her head. He told her:

"I finally let go of the controls."

Terri knew this was the truth.

"Steve had beaten advanced prostate cancer a few years prior to his heart attack, but he lived in fear of it coming back. Thoughts of his cancer haunted him due to intermittent bleeding and pain in his bladder, both a result of radiation damage. I truly believe he willed himself to live. His greatest desire was to see our girls grow up and to make sure we were taken care of. He believed it was his job to provide for all of us. But in those last few months prior to his death, Steve saw me growing deeper in my faith and knowingness that God is the provider, not him. By seeing me stand in this truth and by owning this for himself, I believe Steve was able to release the controls of his life and move to the other side."

What she knew for sure is that he was still watching over his family. The day after he died, she took a walk and once again invited Steve's spirit in. She totally felt his presence and even noticed that he no longer walked with the slight limp he had on earth. When she asked him about it he said, *"There's no pain over here."*

He gave her several more potent messages including one very cryptic one:

"You're going to surround yourself with women."

She had no idea what that meant until she met Charlie Britt. She and Charlie were acquaintances through their daughters' high school dance team. She knew he was a nice man, raising his daughter as a single Dad after his wife of 17 years had committed suicide.

When Steve passed, Charlie extended his hand as a support and a friend. Three months later they began dating and Terri quickly recognized Charlie as a "soulmate."

Now you may be thinking, didn't she feel the need to grieve? What about her kids? Didn't she move too fast? She asked herself these same questions, constantly, and her answer was always the same:

"Terri, let God be the guide."

She realized that for the previous three years, before Steve crossed over, she had been grieving as a result of his advanced cancer diagnosis and surgeries.

During these years they became better friends but due to the nature of his treatment, lost the ability to be intimate, passionate, and romantic.

As part of her healing process, Terri began reading romance novels that inspired her to dream about what her next relationship would be like. She knew, deep within her heart, that she wanted everything she had with Steve plus a lot more passion and romance! And, that's exactly what Charlie brought to the party!

They married 17 months after Steve passed.

When people ask her how she brought such a terrific new guy into her life she has a three-part explanation: God, Steve, and the Law of Attraction.

"I spent years healing my negative beliefs, giving myself permission to honor and love the way I was created. When I finally gave myself permission to have passion in all areas of my life, Charlie arrived," she explains.

"Steve also played an integral part in directing me to Charlie. One night shortly after his death but prior to Charlie and me getting together, a friend mentioned the word 'dating' to me. At first I gasped because dating was the furthest thing from my mind. But then I jumped on an Internet dating site to see what my future prospects were in my small community. Every smoke alarm went off in my home! My kids came running and asked what was going on. 'Nothing is wrong,' I said. 'It's just your dad talking to me.' And I knew it was. He was telling me that a dating site was not where I was heading! And you know what? Once I got that message, every alarm turned off. I didn't have to do a thing to shut them off!"

*"Arielle, I believe Steve was working through you, too. You and I talked right after Charlie and I started dating. I was questioning myself a little because of the suddenness of this new relationship. You sent me a book called **Send Me Someone** by Diana Wentworth. I truly felt Steve gave you the nudge to call me and to send me that book to let me know that he was watching over me. That book helped me know without a doubt that he had sent Charlie to me."*

She still sees and hears from Steve. Recently he explained to her:

"When you get to the other side there is a depth of intimacy and understanding about love. It's not like you are giving love to one and taking from another. It's being in the presence of the love and energy and wholeness so that you feel connected in yourself and to each other. In terms of spending time together, there is no marriage – that's a human thing, it's literally a connection of energy and we can all be together as one. It's more spirit, more essence."

For the past six years, Terri and Charlie blended their families and created a warm and loving home. *"We have three girls, two female dogs, and Charlie and me. I believe that's what Steve's spirit meant when he said I was going to surround myself with women. He was right. What a blessing! We're not perfect by any means. We have our ups and downs like any family but with our girls there are so many gifts. Charlie and I both know that what-ever comes our way, it's a chance for healing our hearts,"* Terri says.

Through their personal and beautiful, inspiring stories, Diana, Kristine, Christina and Terri clearly demonstrate that, even though their soulmate is on the other side, these soulmates are still very active in their lives. These stories are proof that your soulmate will assist you in manifesting new love into your life.

All you need to do is ask and receive.

Unable are the loved to die. For love is immortality.

~Emily Dickinson

Chapter Seven
Asking For Heavenly Help

So how do you place a request for assistance from your loved ones on the other side? There are many ways to reach out to them:

Simply speak out loud to them.

Write them a letter and put it under your pillow or insert the letter into a red or pink helium balloon and literally release it to heaven.

Say daily prayers of gratitude and affirmation thanking them for their assistance.
I have found with Debbie that somehow she can hear my thoughts!

Debbie transitioned on February 17, 2013 and later that year on her birthday, October 1, 2013, Debbie's close friend, James Van Praagh, did a Skype session with me and Mom so we could talk to Debbie. One of the first things Debbie acknowledged was that I had her necklace around my neck and Mom was wearing her watch. Then she said to me, *"Don't get your eyes done."*

Just that morning I had been looking in the mirror at the bags under my eyes, thinking it might be time for a visit to a plastic surgeon. I never even said it out loud to anyone! Now, with this clear message from my sister, I have decided to learn to love my puffy undereyes!

Here's the bottomline:

Your loved ones on the other side want to participate in your life. They want you to be happy, satisfied and content, and it is my understanding that they won't make things happen or interfere with your life unless you ask.

There are so many ways they can send us signs and symbols.

If I see butterflies, I know my sister is here.

If I see hummingbirds, it's my step-father Doc.

Coming across a ladybug is a sure sign my Aunt Pearl is hanging around and rainbows are always showing me that my father, Harvey, is nearby.

One friend says that whenever her kids find pennies on the ground, they know it's a gift from their Dad in heaven.

Bottomline: Just ask!

"Death leaves a heartache no one can heal, love leaves a memory no one can steal."

~From a headstone in Ireland

Chapter Eight
Soulmates In Heaven

On July 2, 2014 our beloved Peggy, our Buddha Mom, made her transition after an unexpected diagnosis of cancer. She died just 31 days after learning the news. Fortunately she passed very quickly, very peacefully, surrounded by our family and friends and with a smile on her face.

On October 28, 2014, I was able to connect with Peggy via Laura Alden Kamm to hear what happened once she left her physical body.

During the reading, the first thing Peggy said to us was that when she passed, someone "ceremoniously" lit candles for her next to the bed – she loved that– she said it was the sweetest send-off ever.

This is exactly what happened. With family and friends surrounding Peggy's bed, our friend, minister Terri Daniel, had us form a circle around the bed while she lit candles, said prayers and did a beautiful ceremony.

Before her last breath Peggy started to feel "beyond tingling" going through her body, and she was wishing she had more time to say goodbye to us all. She was aware of her surroundings but couldn't get her mouth to move to say anything.

"It was as if sparklers and fire-flies were lifting off my body and once I relaxed, it was fun. My body was filled with my 'self,' like a balloon within a balloon. Then I felt my "self" shrink and I knew I was going home," Peggy said about her final moments.

Peggy then explained that she had a very easy passing. She wasn't afraid, she felt everyone's love… although she said "she already missed all of us." In those final moments she opened her heart and "felt a tsunami of love."

During her crossing, she saw my sister Debbie, her second soulmate John, with her husband Wayne standing behind John, her mother, her maternal grandmother, an aunt, a sister, my step-father Doc, her guardian angel, and her traveling angel plus many others.

"It was like lift off. I was then in a park with all my loved ones and it felt safe and felt like home. We all sat together, mostly in silence and I could feel everyone's love," she shared.

I asked her to tell me what her experience is today with John and Wayne.

"On earth, Wayne was always so serious, and with John there was more fun, passion and lightness. Now, I have an even deeper love and respect for Wayne and John is as much fun as ever. When I am not off learning new things I am with both Wayne and John, there is only love, no rivalry… we are all playmates. Even Wayne is now a playmate. He wasn't like that on earth but he is now playful! John and Wayne's love for me gives me a lot of energy. The love that the three of us share together is pure contentment and happiness."

Brian and I are so thrilled to know that Peggy is experiencing

70

so much joy and love with her two soulmates on the other side! We can sense her exuberance and excitement in her new world.

So all is well with Peggy.

Now... what about Debbie? Did she finally find soulmate love in heaven?

Again, I turned to Laura Alden Kamm to bring Debbie in for a reading. As Debbie spoke, a mile a minute as she often did on earth, Laura felt compelled to mention several times that she was quoting Debbie and her potty mouth, verbatim. With much excitement she shared her story:

"My soulmate was there to greet me when I crossed over. My light recognized his light instantly. It was like an explosion of heart energy, it was beyond sexual. It opened up my memory of the many lifetimes we had together and I knew I was home, I knew I was safe and I was so happy to be with him again. I call him David but during our lives together he has had different names including David, Joshua Ben, and Xavier. He chose not to incarnate with me in this lifetime so that he could serve as a guardian and guide for me. I didn't know he was my soulmate and I didn't have any memory of past lives with him.

Now that I am here, I can see and remember the many times he was there for me. He whispered in my ear more often than I would care to remember when I was drunk or stoned. He was the catalyst to the voice in my head to snap out of where I was at. One time he screamed "fucking bloody murder" in my ear when I was wacked out of my mind on a hard tile floor of a public bathroom. This was the moment when I knew I had to get sober or die."

She said that Brian and I showed her that soulmate love, at our level, does exist. That our relationship exemplifies what she and David want next. She admitted that while she was on earth she didn't really believe love like this was possible.

Now she understands all the ways she "fucked my life up." This is what gave her the motivation to teach people and show them how to "lift up from the shit." She also said that she now understands one of the reasons she got cancer was because:

"I always walked around pissed off."

"I purposefully chose to struggle with love and just about everything so I could learn and then pull up other people. My job was to lift people up."

Debbie and David are planning future lifetimes together and *"this time we are going to play. I will come back as a woman, David will be a gentleman and I will be able to love in the body and heart at the same time,"* she proclaimed, before she stepped back into the heavenly realms.

It is now so very clear to me that love never dies. Once we are free of the physical body, and living on the other side, there is another, bigger level of love, greater and grander than anything we can imagine here on earth.

While I am not in any hurry to get to heaven, I am excited to know that one day I will be reunited with my loved ones. And, I am also very clear that when I need their guidance or help, all I have to do is ask!

About My Contributors:

Former Miss USA, Terri Britt, is a love expert, energetic healer, and change agent for women and their families. She is the award-winning author of The Enlightened Mom: A Mother's Guide for Bringing Peace, Love & Light to Your Family's Life. She's been seen on Today, On the Record with Greta van Susteren, Hannity & Colmes, and NBC NY. Terri is a wife, mom, stepmom, mompreneur, inspirational speaker and former television host. Terri's mission is to guide women from emotional chaos to peace, passion, playfulness, miracles and abundance.

Terri says, *"We women have the power to create immense change in our lives and homes. We claim that power when we break the good girl rules and treat ourselves as if we matter. And as we do, we thrive instead of survive and become examples for our loved ones."*

For more information, go to http://TerriBritt.com

Kristine Carlson captivated readers worldwide with her first three bestsellers, *An Hour to Live, An Hour to Love: The True Story of the Best Gift Ever Given, Don't Sweat the Small Stuff in Love* and *Don't Sweat the Small Stuff for Women.*

Expanding on the success of her late husband Dr. Richard Carlson's work, (*Don't Sweat the Small Stuff* series), Kristine has continued to share her message of empowerment, success, emotional strength and love.

Her most recent book, ***Heart Broken Open***, is a courageously honest memoir of her personal journey through the depths of grief and mourning after the sudden and unexpected loss of her husband. This powerful book has gained the attention and earned accolades of readers and media across the globe.

www.kristinecarlson.com and www.dontsweat.com

Laura Alden Kamm

"Laura Alden Kamm's voice of transcendent wisdom and compassion will be heard. Intuitively, she shines a gentle, yet penetrating, light into the darkest recess of our soul, bringing light to our own belovedness."
~Iyanla Vanzant, inspirational author, teacher, & OWN TV host of, Fix My Life

Laura is an internationally respected structural and medical intuitive, author, and spiritual teacher. *"There is nothing she can't see ... she's like a walking MRI"*, says Dr. Mark Hoch.

For more than 30 years, people from over 130 countries have sought Laura's gift, requesting her expert intuitive vision in the fields of medicine, energy medicine and healing, mediumship, business, spirituality, and all aspects of life.

Learn from Laura:
Intuitive Wellness; using your body's inner wisdom to heal.
Audio programs: *Unlocking Your Intuitive Power*; how to read the energy of anything.
Color Intuition; master the energy of color for higher awareness, extraordinary perception, and healing.
www.energymedicine.org

Christina Rasmussen is a bestselling author, speaker and philan-thropist on a crusade to change the way we live after loss. As the founder of **Second Firsts** and **Life Starters** both organizations to help people create a pathway back to life after loss, Christina has helped thousands of people rebuild, reclaim, and relaunch their lives using the power of the human mind.

Her book of the same name — *Second Firsts: Live, Laugh, and Love Again*— aims to take her message even further.

www.secondfirsts.com

Diana von Welanetz Wentworth is the New York Times best-selling author of ten award-winning non-fiction books and the coauthor of two Chicken Soup for the Soul titles. Film rights to her romantic memoir, **Send Me Someone** (St. Martins Press), were purchased by the Lifetime Network.

With her late husband Paul von Welanetz, she hosted a long-running television series and founded the Inside Edge (www.InsideEdge.org), a weekly breakfast forum in Southern California, now in its 29th year, which helped launch the careers of many of the most celebrated authors and speakers of our day including Jack Canfield, Susan Jeffers and Louise Hay. Progressive business eaders still gather at the Inside Edge to discuss new ideas in psychology, science, global issues, success strategies, spiritual awareness, and the arts.

Today, Diana speaks internationally on her newest, and only self-published book, written for the American Heart Association, **Love Your Heart: Follow the Red Thread to a Heart-Centered Life.**

www.DianaWentworth.com

Acknowledgements:

This book exists today at the insistence of my sister, Debbie Ford, who nudged me from the other side that I tell this story. Thank you Debbie for continuing to love and support me. James Van Praagh, Debbie adored you, as do I, you are a gift to our family and the world. Thank you for guiding her to her new home.

Laura Alden Kamm, this book would not have been possible without your clear connection to the other side and your generous and loving support of this project.

To my contributors Diana Wentworth, Kristine Carlson, Terri Britt, and Christina Rasmussen, I am very grateful for your generous sharing of your very personal stories.

To the author whisperer, Linda Sivertsen, your magical ability to reorganize words and sentences is amazing. Thank you for always being there for me. Thank you to Judy O'Beirn and Jenn Gibson of Hasmark for getting me up and running on Create Space.

I am blessed to have a wide circle of friends who lift me up and offer encouragement including Claire Zammit, Carol Allen, Heide Banks, Reverend Laurie Sue Brockway, Divina Infusino, Jai Varadaraj, Becky Robbins, Julie Stroud, Cathy Vartuli, Vivian Glyck, Mike Koenigs, Carla Picardi, Marci Shimoff, Peggy McColl, Marianne Williamson, Jill Mangino, Anita Moorjani, Veena Sidhu, Liz Dawn, Ken Druck, Lisette Osmoss,

Kute Blackson, Lisa Nichols, Jennifer McLean, Sheevaun Moran, Marcia Wieder, Heather Fougnier, Nick Ortner, Leize and David Perlmutter, Colette Baron-Reid, Christine Kriner, Terri Mandell, Cheryl Richardson, and so many others.

Finally, I offer immense love and appreciation to my beautiful mother, Sheila Fuerst, and my soulmate husband and best friend, Brian Hilliard for their endless belief in me.

About Arielle Ford:

Arielle Ford is a leading personality in the personal growth and contemporary spirituality movement. For the past 25 years she has been living, teaching, and promoting consciousness through all forms of media. She is a radio host, relationship expert, speaker, columnist and blogger for the Huffington Post.

Arielle is a gifted writer and the author of eight books including The Soulmate Secret: Manifest the Love of Your Life with the Law of Attraction and Wabi Sabi Love: Finding Perfect Love in Imperfect Relationships. She has been called "The Cupid of Consciousness" and "The Fairy Godmother of Love." For many years she was a literary agent and a prominent book publicist. Her clients included Deepak Chopra, Neale Donald Walsch, Wayne Dyer, Marianne Williamson, don Miguel Ruiz, Gary Zukav, Dr. Dean Ornish, Louise Hay, Joan Borysenko, Jack Canfield and Mark Victor Hansen (Chicken Soup for the Soul) and of course her sister, Debbie Ford.

Today she teaches her Soulmate Secret workshops around the world and online at www.soulmatepassion.com She also hosts the world's largest free online love summits: The Art of Love Series (www.lovesummit.com).

Arielle lives in La Jolla, CA with her husband/soulmate, Brian Hilliard and their feline friends. www.soulmatesecret.com and www.loveontheotherside.com and www.twitter.com/arielleford and www.facebook.com/soulmatesecret

Debbie Ford (1955-2013)

Debbie was a New York Times bestselling author of nine books and an internationally acclaimed teacher, speaker, transformational coach, film-maker and expert in the field of personal transformation. She guided tens of thousands of people to learn to love, trust, and embrace all of who they are. She was a pioneering force in incorporating the study and integration of the human shadow into modern psychological and spiritual practices.

She was the Executive Producer of The Shadow Effect movie, a transformational documentary featuring Deepak Chopra, Marianne Williamson, and other provocative thinkers and beloved teachers. Debbie created The Shadow Process Workshop, considered by many to be the gold standard in psychospiritual experiential work, and she founded The Ford Institute for Transformational Training, the renowned personal and professional training organization which offers emotional and spiritual education based on her body of work to individuals and organizations around the world.

Books:

The Dark Side of the Light Chasers: Reclaiming Your Power, Creativity, Brilliance, and Dreams

Spiritual Divorce: Divorce as a Catalyst for an Extraordinary Life

The Secret of the Shadow: The Power of Owning Your Story

The Right Questions: Ten Essential Questions To Guide You To An Extraordinary Life
The Best Year of Your Life: Dream It, Plan It, Live It

Why Good People Do Bad Things: How to Stop Being Your Own Worst Enemy

The 21-Day Consciousness Cleanse: A Breakthrough Program for Connecting with Your Soul's Deepest Purpose

The Shadow Effect: Illuminating the Hidden Power of Your True Self (with Deepak Chopra and Marianne Williamson)

Courage: Overcoming Fear and Igniting Self-Confidence

Social Media
www.facebook.com/DebbieFordFanPage
www.twitter.com/Debbie_Ford

Website
www.DebbieFord.com

Debbie Ford, Brian Hilliard, Arielle Ford

Photo credit: Doug Ellis

Peggy and Wayne Hilliard

Peggy Hilliard and John Morse

Made in the USA
Monee, IL
16 March 2021